I'm DIFFE And I Know It

BY NIKOLE JONES

This Book Belongs To

_____

My name is Flora Flowers, and I'm different! I have a mother, father, sister, brother, and a dog named Moon.

My family does not look like me, and I don't look like them, but we are happy!

One morning when
I got up for school,
I looked in the mirror and
noticed how different my hair
was from my family's and that
the color of my skin wasn't
the same as theirs.

As my parents dropped me off at school that day, I noticed other kids were talking and whispering about how I didn't look like my family. It made me feel sad.

As I sat in class and daydreamed, I started wondering... why don't I look like the rest of my family?

Was I delivered to them by aliens on a spaceship? Did a stork drop me off at the wrong house?

When I got home from school that afternoon, I asked my mom, "Why am I so different from the rest of the family? Why don't I look like you? All the kids at school look like their parents... why am I so different?"

As we sat down for dinner, my mother explained, "Flora, You are special. Your biological parents, the people who created you, couldn't take care of you and give you everything you needed. But they wanted you to have the best life you could possibly have, even if that meant they couldn't be with you anymore."

A tear rolled down my face as I sat there and tried to understand. I slowly said, "So, they didn't want me?"

My mother said, "Of course they wanted you, but they just couldn't provide for you. Then we got to meet you, and you were so special that we knew we wanted to adopt you and make you a part of our family. When we laid eyes on you for the first time, we knew we would be the perfect family for you, and you would be the perfect daughter for us. We made a promise to care for you and give you all of our love."

I began to wipe my tears away and asked her, "So, you took me in as your own, even though I came from another family?

She smiled and nodded. "Yes, Flora. You are more amazing than we could have ever hoped for, and you've filled our hearts and our family with joy and love."

The next morning,
I woke up feeling a lot better.
Everything suddenly made sense.

As I got ready for school, I looked in the mirror and no longer felt like I didn't belong. I felt accepted, unique, and special. I mean, who gets to be loved by so many people? I felt wanted and treasured. What better feeling is there than that?

My dad called out for me to get in the car for school. For once, I couldn't wait to go because I had a new attitude and understanding of why I was so different.

My parents dropped
me off at school, and I felt
confident and happy!

I walked into my classroom with the biggest smile on my face. I now knew why I was different and not like the rest of my family. The color of our skin or the texture of our hair doesn't matter. What matters is how much we love and care for each other, and that's a good feeling.

We are all different, and that's what makes us special! There is no perfect child or parent, just people whose hearts are choosing to love one another, and LOVE IS ALL WE NEED.

Dedicated to my mother, Kathy,
Susan, Shannon, and all my family,
and to anyone who has ever felt
DIFFERENT.

I'M DIFFERENT AND I KNOW IT
Copyright © 2022 By Nikole Jones
Illustrator: Siriencot

Made in the USA
Columbia, SC
13 October 2024

43534366R00020